Presenting for Success

Impress your management and your clients with quality and effective presentations.

David Hunt

Contents

Introduction

Giving presentations, for whatever reason, is something that is increasingly required in all walks of life. You may be a:

- senior manager presenting a business plan
- sales person presenting your proposal to a prospective client
- marketing person presenting at a conference or in a web seminar, usually called a webinar, webcast or web event
- school teacher, trainer or lecturer or even a student presenting some topic to a class

The ability to present is something that will have an important financial bearing on the success of almost every business, school, government department and even us as individuals. It is therefore, a skill worth developing. Unfortunately, very few organisations devote any time or budget to helping their staff or students become proficient in this capability and lose revenue, personal income or graduation marks as a result.

I have sat through many hundreds of pretty tedious presentations and a handful of excellent ones. I have been fortunate to have worked for several businesses that have invested in presentation training. I have also been fortunate in having access to advanced technology for delivering online seminars, or webinars as they are usually called.

Whilst not everyone has the personality or confidence to stand up in front of an audience, or sit down to communicate via the internet to a remote audience; many will still be required to do so.

Anyone can give a quality, effective and professional presentation; you just need to follow the simple guidance given in this short book. If you do, you should never give a poor presentation again.

The objective of this book is not to try and teach people any form of acting skills or take people outside their comfort zones. It is to help you make your deliverances professional and more interesting to your audience to maximise the positive impact and impression you leave them with. Your reputation and confidence will rise as a result.

This book will provide you with some practical, pragmatic and simple steps you can take so that you can present the right image of yourself and your organisation.

Why are you presenting?

The first things to consider are why are you giving a presentation and what does your audience expect?

Whilst it is important that you give a professional and quality impression, you are of secondary importance to your audience. There is an old adage that the customer is king. Well, in a presentation scenario the audience is king!

You may have specific messages you wish to give out to your audience or you may have a specific action you wish attendees to take as a result of your presentation. However, unless you present in a way your audience will understand and be receptive to, you will fail. The style and content may vary depending on your objectives, some examples of which are outlined below.

Marketing
- Improve brand awareness
- Generate sales leads
- Promote customer loyalty by:
  - providing privileged and advance information about future product updates
  - encouraging customers to share experiences, hints and tips
  - soliciting feedback on your products and service performance
  - offering loyalty promotional offers

Sales	▪ Demonstrate product capabilities
	▪ Present a proposal
	▪ Close a deal
Training	▪ Show customers, or prospective customers, how to use a product or service
	▪ Introduce customers to new features so they can enhance their return on existing investments
Support	▪ "How to" sessions to show how to get round, or overcome, a problem using your products or services
Press / Customer / Analyst briefings	▪ Major product launch
	▪ Major company announcements such as acquisitions, mergers or divestments
	▪ Annual meeting of the shareholders
Internal meetings	▪ Present business plans
	▪ Lead brainstorm sessions
School / University teaching	▪ Educate students
	▪ Stimulate discussions

12 key ingredients

Having personally attended hundreds of presentations, presented at dozens of conferences and run more than 300 webinars; I have identified 12 key ingredients for success.

Presentations, whether to a live face-to-face audience at a client's premises, at a business or trade conference or via a webinar don't just happen and are not effective unless they are planned and executed professionally. So here I would like to introduce key ingredients 1-3, often referred to as the "3 Ms of marketing":

- **M**arket
- **M**essage
- **M**edia

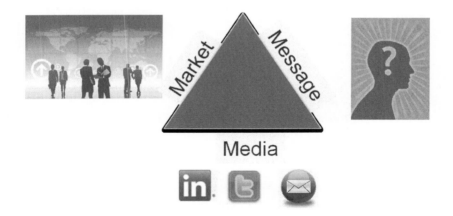

1. Message

If you are not a marketing person you may think that this does not apply to you. Well, whatever the type of presentation or reason for it, every presenter needs to worry about the message. Not just presenting the correct message or information but doing so in a manner your audience will appreciate and that achieves your objectives.

For you to position your message correctly you need to pay heed to the market – your target audience. Someone somewhere needs to take ownership for identifying the market for your presentation.

Someone also needs to ensure your market is aware of your presentation and needs to choose the most appropriate mechanism to inform them about it, otherwise you will have no audience. There is little point preparing and giving a great presentation if there is no one to hear and see it.

Even if only one person turns up to hear your presentation, you owe it to them, to yourself and to your organisation to still put on your best performance and ensure you put across your message to the best of your ability.

2. Market

Just like any marketing activity you need to identify your target market and make sure your messaging is appropriate to attract people to your event.

If you are presenting at a business conference or trade show, the organisers will take care of marketing the event to relevant people; be they business managers, industry specialists, consumers or other interested parties. Your organisation may also want to initiate additional marketing to encourage the right audience to attend your specific presentation.

I don't just mean identifying the industry sector, geographic area or even job title; but do you have a database of relevant contacts?

Maybe, you need to buy one in or use a telemarketing agency to build your target database. These can all prove to be very costly, with no guarantee of accuracy or quality. Nonetheless, this needs careful consideration if you are to have the right individuals in your audience and sufficient numbers of them to make the effort and costs worthwhile.

If you are presenting as part of a sales effort to win business for your company, the salesperson may take responsibility for ensuring the right people have been identified to attend your presentation.

Whatever the reason, someone will need to ensure the right attendees (market) have been identified.

3. Media

Having identified your target market and agreed the appropriate message, someone needs to ensure the relevant people are made aware of your presentation. They will need to consider the most appropriate media to use to reach your intended audience.

If the target audience is known to you or your organisation, a personal invitation by telephone, letter or email may do the trick.

If you are running a marketing event to promote your brand and find potential new customers, it may be more economical and more successful to adopt mass emailing and / or use combinations of social media such as Twitter, LinkedIn and Facebook to spread the word.

There are many books and training courses on the use of social media and email broadcasting. This book will therefore not go into this area in any more detail.

4. Preparation

Whatever you do, do not leave preparation until the last moment. Unless you are very skilful at preparing and giving presentations your lack of preparation will be apparent to your audience, who will

rightly question that if you could not be bothered to make their attendance worthwhile; why should they be bothered to do business with you?

As a presenter it is your responsibility to ensure you understand the target audience and the message(s) you need to give. It is your responsibility to prepare your presentation so that your audience enjoys it and values the time they spent listening to you.

The next chapter will provide specific tips to improve the quality and value of your presentations, even if the thought of giving one fills you with dread. If you have given many presentations over the years, the chances are you are one of the 99% who have fallen into bad practices. If the latter applies, you may also find these simple tips most beneficial as you will be able to take corrective action for the future.

5. Rehearsal

Would you ever attend a production at the theatre and expect them to give their performance without any rehearsals? Of course not.

This is equally important for your presentations. **More** important, really, as you will probably not be used to performing to an audience; especially one you cannot see if you are presenting via a

webinar.

There is a saying that practice makes perfect. The more presentations you give; the more confident and proficient you will become.

There are often opportunities to present to a friendly and helpful audience at your place of work. I would strongly encourage you, your colleagues and your staff to volunteer for giving presentations internally, so you can practice the skills and techniques in this book. This will help you gain confidence and quality; ensuring you portray the right image of yourself and your organisation, when called upon to present to the outside world.

6. Event Management

It is a good idea to have someone take charge of both hosting the event and managing the process. That way you as the presenter can concentrate on delivering your presentation without having to worry about logistics, facilities or the technology involved.

Too many presentations are ruined when something unexpected happens, or otherwise does not happen as expected. Technology does not always work as we expect. Not all issues can be resolved instantly, of course, but having an experienced person at the helm can often help overcome them with little to no detrimental effect for the audience.

In order to concentrate fully on the delivery of your presentation, it is good practice to have a colleague assist with any additional aspects involved. For example:

Type of event	Typical Management Needs
Presentation to a large, face-to face audience such as at a business conference or press briefing etc.	▪ Audience registration ▪ Seating ▪ Data projector ▪ Audio requirements
Small face-to-face event such as a sales presentation to potential client management.	▪ Briefings re attendees ▪ Room layout ▪ Presentation facilities ▪ Introductions

Webinars / Online events

- Hosting the event
- Technology needs
- Technical issues
- Monitoring Q&A or chat
- Conducting polls

7. Delivery

 Some aspects of delivery will be expanded upon in the next chapter; however there are some key golden rules you must obey when delivering your presentation. You will probably recognise and relate to many of these from presentations you have endured. Make sure you yourself are not guilty of the following:

Not being clear about what you are going to say.

Please avoid 'ers' and 'ums' whilst talking; it is a most annoying habit. Be clear what you want to say before you say it, so you can do so without hesitation.

Mumbling

Always speak clearly and loud enough for everyone in your audience to hear what you are saying.

Non-stop delivery

Some presenters are so nervous, excited or enthusiastic that they speak very quickly. They forget to pause between sentences or after they have made an important point. A good way to emphasise the importance of what is being said, is to pause before and after key statements.

Silence can be very powerful. Do not be afraid to pause for several seconds – count to 5 or even 10 slowly in your head. It may seem like a lifetime the first time you try it, but I assure you your audience will be listening. This pause will allow them to actually think about what you have just said, and listen more intently to what you say next.

Annoying habits

How often have you been distracted by a presenter who repeatedly scratches himself, pulls at an ear, jangles coins or keys in his pocket?

Being afraid to be controversial

A good way to get the attention of your audience is to start off with a controversial, intriguing or humorous statement that you will come back to at the end of your presentation.

Not daring to be different

Think of your poor audience, especially if they have sat through several tedious presentations. How can you make yours stand out and be more memorable? We will expand on this in the next chapter with presentation dos and don'ts.

Reading your slides

If you just read your slides you are insulting your audience and there is very little point to you actually being there. Your audience will most likely read the slides at a different pace to you, so may not fully digest what you are saying.

Likewise, they may find it frustrating if you are taking longer than necessary when they have read the slide more quickly than you.

Turning your back on your audience

Even worse than reading your slides verbatim is turning your back on the audience to read from the screen. Not only is this amateurish and disrespectful for your audience; they might slip out of the room without you noticing!

In summary you need to:

- Get their attention
- Communicate well and clearly
- Avoid waffle
- Keep your audience interested and involved

8. Interaction

Unless the objective is for you to deliver a one-directional monologue, as in a political delivery of a speech; it is good practice

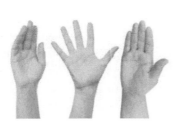

to interact with your audience. Asking questions to elicit feedback is good. Asking for a show of hands works well too. Always encourage your audience to ask questions but do give clear guidance as to whether you will take questions during the presentation or at the end.

It is often a good idea to request that questions be kept until the end unless it is to seek clarification on something you have said that otherwise would leave them confused. Inexperienced presenters are easily side-tracked by curveball questions. Addressing such questions mid-session can be problematic, as they may totally destroy both your flow and your message and may cause you to run out of time before completing your presentation.

By taking questions at the end you will be better able to control your flow, ensure your messages are delivered correctly and professionally. You can then relax, knowing you are managing your time effectively; whilst continuing on to take as many questions as the remaining time allows.

When asked questions though, do listen carefully (or read carefully if it is an online webinar) and THINK before you answer. This is especially important to make sure you don't say something that is inaccurate or could subsequently be damaging to your reputation or your business.

If you need a few moments to consider the question carefully and formulate your answer, simply tell your audience that you need to think about that one for a while. Once you are ready and have thought of your response, then give it. This is far better than starting to ramble on in the hope that some sensible words eventually come out of your mouth.

9. Time-keeping

Unless there are exceptional reasons to contradict this, you should always aim to start and finish on time. You should show respect for your audience and the time they are devoting to attend your presentation. So, if your session is scheduled for forty-five minutes, make sure you can deliver the content within that time; including allowing for some questions at the end.

Ingredients 10 – 12 relate to the follow-up relating to your presentation.

10. Thank you

Do remember to thank those who attended your presentation; you should do so as a matter of course at the end of the session. It is also courteous and good sales practice to follow up with a letter, email or telephone call to those who attended. This will allow you to solicit feedback or agreement to any actions you may be seeking as a result of the presentation.

It is also good practice to follow up with those that had registered for the session but did not, for whatever reason, attend. The fact they had registered indicates they had an interest in your topic. It is possible they have a problem that your business can solve, or perhaps have another interest in talking to you.

If your event was delivered by way of a webinar, there is a good chance your webinar service includes an automated "thank you for attending" or "sorry we missed you" email facility to assist this process.

11. Presentation feedback

It is a good idea to elicit feedback from attendees so you can gauge whether or not there is a good level of interest in your subject matter. This is also beneficial as it will allow

you to find out how you can improve future events or presentations that you give.

If you are in a face-to-face event such as at a conference, you will have greater success with this if you ask attendees to complete a feedback form before they leave the room. Offering an incentive such as a prize draw will often have the desired effect of increasing response rates.

If you are using an online webinar you could conduct a poll before you end the event. You will be limited, though, to just one or two questions as attendees won't hang around once you have finished. Another option is to direct them to a feedback questionnaire link when they leave the event or via your follow-up "thank you" email.

12. Ongoing Q&A

Finally, if any attendees did raise questions that you were unable or unwilling to answer, make sure you do get in touch with them afterwards to provide feedback to the questions they had raised.

So there we have it; the 12 key ingredients for a successful presentation.

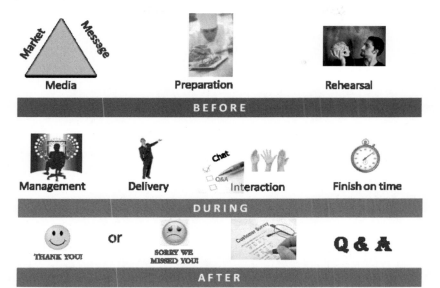

Presentation content dos and don'ts

So, having helped you to address the 12 key ingredients for a successful presentation; let us now turn our attention to the actual content.

The intention here is not to tell you what you should present, as I could not possibly know what that may be. What I can do however, is provide some simple tips that will greatly improve the quality of your slides and the effect they will have on your audience.

I am sure many readers have attended conferences where you have sat through presentation after presentation and suffered "death by PowerPoint". Many people criticise Microsoft® PowerPoint for this. Well, it is not the fault of PowerPoint; it is the fault of the lazy and unskilled people who created the slides and delivered the presentations. They failed to think of their audience. These simple tips should ensure you are not guilty of such a death.

Avoid long sentences

Are you guilty of slides like this example below?

- **Please avoid writing lots of text on slides in long sentences. Whilst putting everything on the slide means you don't have to memorise what you want to say, it makes your slides boring and you will lose your audience as they will either read the slide and switch off, or worse still, switch off before taking in the very important information you have put on the slide.**
- **If you have lots of information on the slide and merely read it out, there is no point you being there to present it, and you insult the intelligence of the audience.**

Too many presenters use slides such as this.

Not only will you bore your audience but unless you are adding significant additional information with your verbal content, there is no point to you actually being there to present the slides. Your audience could read the presentation any time that they choose, or more likely, they simply won't bother.

On the other hand, if you are seeking to add valuable, supporting information verbally; your audience may not take it in if there is too much distracting information on the screen. An overwhelming level of detail can be hugely counterproductive as it will take the audience's attention away from what you are saying.

Avoiding long sentences on your slides is probably one of the single most beneficial changes you can make.

Don't read the slides

Some people fall into an even bigger trap. They not only have all the information on the slide and proceed to read it word for word, they try to justify their presence by repeating each sentence using slightly different words that add nothing to the information and frustrate the audience.

I have sat though too many such presentations and, once I have read the slide, I just want the presenter to move to the next one quickly as I am bored and frustrated. Please, please, please don't do this to your audience – especially if I am in it!

Avoid overly complicated diagrams

A picture paints a thousand words and I strongly advocate the use of pictures and diagrams instead of verbiage on the slides.

However, it seems to be compulsory in technology marketing presentations to include overly complex technical architecture diagrams.

These either contain far too much information or require clear explanation that too often is not presented.

To avoid embarrassing any individual technology company, I have chosen a totally different example of a diagram that might not prove too helpful in a presentation.

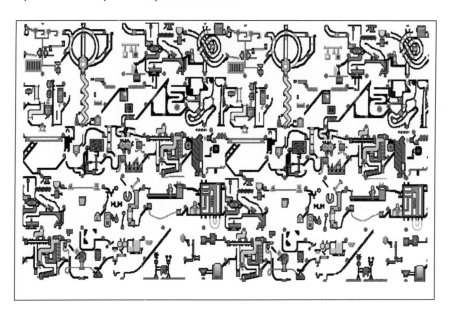

A picture should assist the understanding, or help to retain the viewer's interest, by encouraging them to listen to what you are saying.

For example, if you are giving a talk on the behaviour patterns of flamingos, it would be very helpful and effective to show a picture of such behaviour, for attendees to see whilst you are pointing out the characteristics to which you wish to draw their attention.

Don't shoot your audience with bullets!

Another common failing by many presenters is to rely far too heavily on bullet points; although certainly, they have their use.

Again you need to think of your audience. How many conferences have you attended where you have suffered presentation after presentation full of bullet-point slides?

- **Slide after slide of bullets is boring**
- **Use different styles**
- **How many presentations have you sat through with lots of slides just like this?**
- **I bet it is quite a few**
- **Your eyes glaze over after a while**

Use interesting and relevant pictures wherever possible, as in the flamingo example above. If there are no suitable pictures that would assist with your presentation and you feel you have no option but to use bullets; I suggest you make use of the SmartArt facility in PowerPoint, to enable you to present bullet style information in a more visually attractive format. You just select your preferred diagram style and enter your "bullets". PowerPoint will turn them into an attractive diagram.

Do remember though NOT to use full sentences; keywords should be sufficient. They will encourage your audience to listen to what you have to say and will act as a memory jogger afterwards, if they review any handout copies of your slides.

Do spoll-chick your slides!

Nothing detracts from presentation content more than spelling errors. They make you look unprofessional and your audience WILL notice them. Their concentration will switch from your important content to your spelling error(s). The spell-checker is there for a reason. Please use it.

Dare to be different

I cannot over-emphasise the importance of the audience and how you should always consider them when preparing your presentation.

Many years ago I was amongst many managers who were asked to attend a business planning meeting. We were all asked to present our business plans to our peers and senior management team.

We had been provided with a fixed template that we were to use. It contained slide after slide of business strategy headings and sales projections.

A good many business plans had been reviewed before my slot. My chances of receiving much attention at that stage were low and their eyes were already glazing over. As the management were largely American, I started off with a short quiz on the meanings of various cockney rhyming slang phrases.

That injected some humour into the proceedings and life into the management team. I then presented my business plan purely as pictures to identify the challenges and how I planned to address them. This went down very well, even though I had not followed the compulsory format, and this made for much more interesting discussions afterwards.

I have known presenters ask their attendees to stand up and jump up and down quickly several times to ensure they were awake!

If you have any particular skills or talent, such as a modicum of proficiency in magic, you might perform a trick or two with members of the audience. This can work particularly well if you can relate it back to the topic.

If you are presenting on IT security, your audience would probably expect that you will talk about security issues and risks from the Security Officer's point of view. However, if you were to present it from a hacker or fraudster's perspective, you would make your audience think about the issues rather differently. This might make your messages more memorable; especially if you involved an ex-fraudster as part of your presentation. I have seen this done and it was most effective.

Recommended viewing

There is a great video available on YouTube by a comedian called Dan McMillan. It is called "Life after death by PowerPoint". It lasts less than 5 minutes and I recommend every presenter to watch this short video BEFORE they prepare their slides.

There is a link to it from the useful tips section of my website: www.thewebeventscompany.com/presentation-tips.

Product demonstration dos and don'ts

Before you perform any product demonstration, you need to be very clear as to your objectives.

If, for example, you are showing off your latest kitchen gadget at a consumer show, you may want to show every single clever (in your mind) thing your gadget can do. Things that no one realised they had a problem doing, allowing you to bamboozle the easily impressed members of the crowd into parting with their cash before they actually switch on their brains and realise they will never use it more than once. After they try it at home for the first time they realise it takes longer to take all the components apart to wash them than it would have taken you to perform the task without this product.

If you are in a more professional business to business environment, you will probably be giving a demonstration for one of two main reasons:

- To spark interest from your audience, allowing a salesperson to then follow-up, in order to try to generate a sale.

- To demonstrate to a prospective customer that your product solves specific needs, that the customer is looking to address.

In the first case, your demonstration should be kept simple. If your product has ten different ways of doing something, don't show all ten. This will confuse the audience and make your product seem complicated. It is often a good idea to pick on one or two key problems that your potential customers are likely to have, then show how easily your product can solve them.

In the second scenario you should be very clear what problems your potential customer has expressed. Your demonstration should then be highly focused to prove you can meet his needs. Be very wary of doing a feature dump of things that are not relevant, as they may make your product seem too complicated. You might also introduce your customer to weaker aspects of your product, which may not compare favourably with those presented by a competitor.

Once you have decided what you will demonstrate, there are some very basic rules you can follow to maximise the positive impact your demonstration will give. Some of these are specific to computer software demonstration, others are more generic, but I offer them for your consideration.

These are in addition to the presentation guidelines provided in the chapter "12 key ingredients."

Agree roles   Be very clear who will do what during the demonstration / meeting. In a sales demonstration, the sales representative will be in charge and will typically:

- Do the introductions

- Summarise or present the customer situation, problems and confirm what you will demonstrate

- Ensure the audience has understood the benefits of what you have demonstrated

- Manage any Q&A

- Summarise and agree the follow-up / next steps

Have clear objectives	When you are asked to give a demonstration, you should be briefed sufficiently in advance. You should then prepare as appropriate in order to ensure it specifically addresses the needs of the audience whilst following a clear and logical path.
Understand the technology	Make sure you really do know how your software works. If you as the specialist don't understand it thoroughly, how will your customers ever be able to?
	If you are using any technology for the first time – a new data projector or some webinar facility - do have a trial run beforehand to ensure you don't make a fool of yourself in front of your prospective customers.
Sound interesting	Be enthusiastic about your product. If you can't, who can? Make sure you alter the tone of your voice so the audience wants to listen to you and likewise enjoys listening to you.
	Listening to a monotone for an hour is a great way of solving someone's insomnia and losing a sale!

Involve the audience & seek regular feedback

After each section of your demonstration, especially if intended to prove you can meet the customer's needs; do seek confirmation that they agree your product has addressed their requirements and they like what you have shown.

If your product really is easy, invite the customers to try it for themselves – under your clear guidance and instructions, of course. If they do something for themselves, like produce a complex report in seconds that used to take them several days to produce manually, it will make them really pleased with your product. They will experience first-hand, just how much time your solution will save them.

But don't allow questions to destroy your flow.

Whilst it is important to answer questions that seek clarification of a particular point, if you become embroiled in a series of follow-on questions or discussion it can destroy your time-plan and the delivery of your key message. It may also be boring for other members of the audience, so they lose interest or even leave the session.

Keep within the time schedule

Avoid running out of time before you have shown the most important feature; the one you wanted to wow them with at the end of your session. If this happens, you have missed your chance and wasted the opportunity offered by the prospective client.

Keep to the point	Only demonstrate what needs to be demonstrated, unless the sales person suggests or agrees to going off-plan.
Listen carefully	Do not start answering questions before your customer has finished asking them. Not only is it annoying for the customer, you might easily misunderstand the nature of what he was really asking.
Relate to the customer	If you are unable to directly simulate your client's business scenario within your demonstration, do make sure you relate each aspect to their situation. ..." so when your AP clerk does this you will immediately see an alert on your screen," for example.
Avoid rapid mouse movements	Many software demonstrators move the mouse frantically around the screen whilst they are talking; this is most distracting. When you need to move the mouse, do so slowly so your audience can see what you are doing. If you don't need to move the mouse, take your hand off it.
Don't let technical issues undermine your product	If you come across a bug in the software, do NOT repeat what you have done, you will only reproduce the bug. If you experience any technical issues that require you to spend time fixing it by rebooting your computer for example, switch off the projector so the audience does not see what jiggery-pokery you have to go though to get things working. This can otherwise leave a very poor impression of your product.

Whilst you are doing this, some other member of your team should be engaging the customer in the beneficial aspects of your product. This will help to keep the audience in a positive frame of mind, for when you resume your demonstration.

Event economics

As many readers will be seeking to hone their presentation skills due to involvement in marketing or lead generation activities; I will now turn briefly to the economics involved in different types of events at which you may consider presenting.

Unless you are regarded as a specialist or leader in your field, obtaining a presentation slot at a business conference or exhibition will often be dependent on your business actively supporting the event through sponsorship and the purchase of exhibition space.

In this chapter therefore I will look at the economics of a number of real-life, lead-generation activities undertaken by a number of companies in:

- an international business conference
- a UK business conference
- a UK trade exhibition
- a private UK breakfast briefing
- two different types of online webinars

The analysis performed addressed the true total cost per lead generated. Too many business people fail to take into consideration the total costs involved in certain activities. As a result, they end up making ill-judged decisions that seem the best financial option up front but in reality represent very poor value for money. The real life examples overleaf serve to confirm this.

All monetary values are in UK pounds sterling.

	Int'l Conference	UK Conference	UK Trade Show	London Seminar	Webinar 1	Webinar 2
Cost of booth	7,813	6,750	4,500	0	0	0
Cost of display stand[1]	400	400	200	200	0	0
No. of staff	6	3	2	6	1	1
Total staff days[2]	42	8	6	8	1	1
Daily staff costs[3]	250	250	250	500	500	500
Total staff costs	10,500	2,000	1,500	4,000	500	500
Travel	7,900	300	250	150	0	0
Hotel	10,080	1,350	450	0	0	0
Expenses	1800	200	140	0	1,950	1,500
Sponsorships	10,000	0	0	700	0	0
Other costs[4]	1,000	500	150	100	0	0
Total cost of event	49,493	11,500	7,190	5,150	2,450	2,000
No. of visitors	70	60	20	25	8	83
Real leads[5]	5	12	10	2	5	70
Cost per lead	**£9,899**	**£958**	**£719**	**£2,575**	**£490**	**£29**

Notes for the above table:

1 Assumes display costs are written off over 5 events

2 Excludes event preparation time for conferences / shows

3 The differences in daily staff costs are due to senior (Director level) participants at some events

4 Includes supply or hire of electric power, plasma displays, lead scanners and such like

5 Those who visited the stand or event for reasons other than to take part in prize draw and who had a genuine interest in the products or services offered!

As you can see in the table, the cost per lead varied from £29 to £9,899. In other words the Webinar represented a saving in excess of 99%!

Without a doubt the webinar approach proved to be a far more economic way of generating new sales opportunities. The main difference in the relative success factors (and cost per lead) between the two different types of webinar was due to the quality of the contact data available for the invitation process. This made a significant impact on the number and relevance of attendees.

This analysis has concentrated purely on the costs per lead generated. However, there may be other reasons why you still decide to participate in certain quality exhibitions or conferences. You may, for example, be able to meet up with partners, suppliers or other attendees who would not attend a Webinar you arrange. Only you can determine the value of that to your business or organisation.

Are webinars effective?

The well respected marketing organisation, Marketing Profs, conducted research for its report "9 management practices for exceptional webinars". The primary reasons companies run Webinars are shown in the chart below.

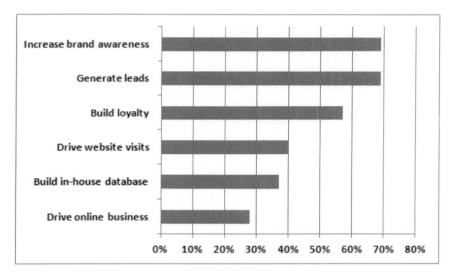

The report goes on to state that the benefit improves over time with companies who have been running them for more than 3 years, finding them more effective than those conducting webinars for less than a year. Furthermore, those who conduct six or more webinars per year find them more effective at generating quality leads than those who conduct fewer.

Webinars are popular with a wide variety of businesses for one simple reason; they work. They do so for the following reasons:

- You can reach out to potential or existing customers and partners irrespective of geography.

- You can establish dialog with each individual attendee by means of the chat and Q&A facilities. People who might be too shy to raise a question in open forum in a face-to-face seminar feel more comfortable doing so in an on-line environment.

- They are a very economical way of communicating to an audience, large or small.

- You can make Webinar recordings available to those who could not attend the live event.

The testimonials overleaf are from clients, who have used my personal webinar services. They would certainly agree with the above and clearly believe they are an effective way to market their businesses and generate new sales opportunities.

Client Testimonials

"As a Sales person who needed as many good leads as possible, the most efficient way to create leads has been David's webinars."

- European Sales Manager

"I would highly recommend The WebEvents Company to run webinars and create leads."

- Sales Manager, Europe & South America

"From the initial event conception through to the actual webinar's delivery and post event follow-up; everything was always organised smoothly and professionally."

- European Sales Manager

"David is an extremely efficient and meticulous marketing person, who is absolutely excellent in running Webinars. With flawless execution expertise, David makes webinars look like a cakewalk!"

- Senior Manager, Marketing

"I tried to run one webinar myself and experienced a number of problems. I now know this requires a unique skill that only David has!"

- Sales Manager

"David brought the professionalism and experience we needed to our webinars. I would recommend David running anyone's webinars moving forward."

- Business Development Manager, UK & South Africa

A final thought

If the information and suggestions contained in this book help you to give a better presentation, secure that new job or help you win that promotion or win just one sale; what value can you place on that?

This could be the best value book you have ever bought!

About the author

David Hunt is the Managing Director of The **WebEvents** Company and the Principal Partner at Interimco.

David is a sales and marketing professional with 30+ years operating at senior management level. He has been asked to present at numerous conferences around the world and has run and presented in more than 300 webinars.

Having enjoyed an excellent corporate career working for leading companies such as ADP, Digital (DEC) and Microsoft; David founded Interimco in 1998 to work as an independent change and transition leader. In 2012 he founded The **WebEvents** Company to enable businesses of all sizes to benefit from his webinar and presentation experience. He achieves this by offering a bespoke, all-inclusive, fixed-price webinar service; with the assurance of his personalised and unsurpassed attention to detail.

If you would like further information on any of the above, please visit www.TheWebEventsCompany.com and www.Interimco.co.uk.

Personal notes